Platform
Papers

Quarterly essays from Currency House   No. 7: January 2006

CURRENCY HOUSE

PLATFORM PAPERS

Quarterly essays from Currency House Inc.

Editor: Dr John Golder, j.golder@unsw.edu.au

Currency House Inc. is a non-profit association and resource centre advocating the role of the performing arts in public life by research, debate and publication.

Postal address: PO Box 2270, Strawberry Hills, NSW 2012, Australia
Email: info@currencyhouse.org.au   Tel: (02) 9319 4953
Website: www.currencyhouse.org.au   Fax: (02) 9319 3649

Executive Officer: Eamon Flack

Editorial Board: Katharine Brisbane AM, Dr John Golder,
    John McCallum, Greig Tillotson

ISBN 0 9757301 3 4
ISSN 1449-583X

Cover design by Kate Florance
Typeset in 10.5 Arrus BT
Printed by Hyde Park Press, Adelaide

This edition of Platform Papers is supported by donations from the following: Katharine Brisbane, Malcolm Duncan, David Marr, Tony Scotford, Alan Seymour, Greg and Fiona Quirk, Mary Vallentine and Jane Westbrook. To them and to all our supporters Currency House extends sincere gratitude.

Contents

AVAILABILITY   *Platform Papers*, quarterly essays on the
performing arts, is published every January, April, July
and October and is available through bookshops or by
subscription (for order form, see page 70).

LETTERS   Currency House invites readers to submit letters
of 400–1,000 words in response to the essays. Letters should
be emailed to the Editor at j.golder@unsw.edu.au or posted
to Currency House at PO Box 2270, Strawberry Hills, NSW
2012, Australia. To be considered for the next issue, the
letters must be received by 18 February 2006.

CURRENCY HOUSE   For membership details, see our
website at: www.currencyhouse.org.au

Does Australia Need a Cultural Policy?

DAVID THROSBY

Author's acknowledgements

This essay is dedicated to the memory of Donald Horne. There is much in these pages with which I'm sure he would take issue, but he would see that that is as it should be. He would probably be sceptical about proposals for a cultural policy, but he would undoubtedly relish the prospect of discussing the arguments for and against. It is a curious conundrum that he was dubious about the idea of such a concept as Australian identity, yet he manifested in himself and in his writings much of the best of what Australia was, is and can become.

With the usual *caveat*, I am grateful to Clive Bean, Richard Eckersley, Murray Goot and Clive Hamilton for providing materials that were helpful to me in the writing of this essay

The author

DAVID THROSBY is internationally known for his work
in the economics of arts and culture. He is Professor
of Economics at Macquarie University and his field of
research and writing has included the economic role
of artists, the economics of public intervention in arts
markets, cultural development, cultural policy, heritage
issues and the sustainability of cultural processes. His
books include *The Economics of the Performing Arts*
(with Glenn Withers, Melbourne: Edward Arnold 1979)
and *Economics and Culture* (Cambridge: Cambridge
University Press 2001). He has produced several studies
for the Australia Council, including *But What Do You Do
for a Living? A New Economic Study of Australian Artists*
(with Beverley Thompson, 1994) and *Don't Give Up
Your Day Job: an Economic Study of Professional Artists
in Australia* (with Virginia Hollister, 2003).

He has been a consultant to the World Bank,
the OECD, FAO and UNESCO and in 1990–93 chaired
three Prime Minister's Working Groups on ecologically
sustainable development. He is a past President of the
Association for Cultural Economics International, and
was Foundation Chair of the National Association for
the Visual Arts. He has served on the boards of the
Australian Museum, the Museum of Contemporary Arts,
the Copyright Agency Ltd and VISCOPY. He is also a

member of the editorial boards of the *Journal of Cultural Economics*, the *International Journal of Cultural Policy, Poetics* and the *Pacific Economic Bulletin*.

David Throsby has also written several plays, one of which (*The Number-One Rooster*) was produced at the Royal Court Theatre, London, in 1975.

He was elected a Fellow of the Academy of Social Sciences in Australia in 1988.

1
What is cultural policy?

Google, like Glad Wrap, is something we didn't know we needed until we got it, and now we've got it we can't do without it. The process of googling can give us insight and information about anything at all. Could it help us to define what is meant by 'cultural policy'? Try it. At last count, entering these words into that seductive rectangular space produced 372,000 hits. Clearly, cultural policy is alive and well, at least in cyberspace. It's doing OK in scholar-space too—a search using the academic version of Google gives around 5,120 hits for 'cultural policy', spanning books and journals in economics, sociology, arts management, cultural studies and political science.

This essay asks what cultural policy is and how policy towards the arts and culture has evolved in Australia over time. The most ambitious attempt to formulate an explicit cultural policy by any federal government was the ALP's *Creative Nation* statement of 1994. I want to discuss the origins of this document and such legacy as it has had, in order to ask whether, after a decade of the Howard Government, the time is not ripe for a renewed effort to set out a cultural policy for this country. If it is, then what should such a policy look like? To begin with we need to understand what the term 'cultural policy' embraces.

Despite the avalanche of information about cultural policy unearthed by Google, defining it remains problematical. Maybe the clearest thing we can say with certainty is that we know what it's not. No one in an open democratic society such as the one we are supposed to inhabit would see cultural policy as the formal imposition of state culture on the population—that is, a situation in which our political masters tell us what our culture is or should be. This is precisely the situation depicted, for example, in David Pownall's *Master Class*; at one point in this brilliant play, which is set in the former USSR, Stalin's Minister for Culture reminds Prokofiev and Shostakovich of the decree handed down by the Central Committee of the Communist Party proclaiming that 'Soviet composers must become more conscious of their duties to the People and stimulate the kind of creative activity that will lead to higher-quality works being composed which will be worthy of the Soviet people'.[1] This sort of verbally-challenged diktat may work in totalitarian regimes of both right and left, but not here.

If we look to other countries' cultural policies as an aid to definition, we find considerable variations around the world. Here are just three examples.[2] First, the Canadian Government has described its cultural policy in the following terms:

> Canada's cultural fabric has been shaped by a small and geographically dispersed population, limited

economies of scale and high costs of production, the ubiquitous proximity and presence of the United States of America (the world's largest and most influential cultural super-power) and a unique blend of multicultural demographics, official linguistic duality (French and English) and diverse Aboriginal cultures. The development of a national cultural policy for Canada by the federal government has therefore been shaped largely by the need to protect and affirm Canadian cultural sovereignty and to promote national unity and a Canadian identity.

The second example is from France, where the history of cultural policy from its origins under royal patronage until the present day has been marked by the central role played by the State in promoting and organising the idea of French arts, language and culture through the great national cultural institutions, performing companies, academies and government-supported cultural programs. The Ministry of Culture has had fiscal and administrative responsibility for implementation of the national cultural policy which nowadays covers heritage protection, contemporary artistic creation, dissemination and training, and the regulation of cultural industry markets. Finally, in the United Kingdom, cultural policy has been strongly focussed on support for the arts, a deliberate strategy at least since the 1940s. But at a broader level its goals are to increase access to, and participation in, the cultural and sporting life of the nation and to enhance the quality of the experience on offer, cultivating an appetite for excellence. British cultural policy is also directed towards promoting good design, fostering education in the arts and culture, facilitating the role of the arts in urban revitalisation, and developing the creative industries.

These examples illustrate the fact that, even though there are common elements amongst them, defining cultural policy in terms of actual experience around the world won't lead to a single answer. So, as an alternative we could try going back to first principles, and attempting to define culture itself. This turns out to be no less problematical. Robert Borofsky once said that defining culture was akin to 'encaging the wind',[3] a statement that reflects the elusive nature of culture, deriving as it does from so many different facets of human experience. Nevertheless, it is remarkable how widely the word 'culture' is used nowadays in common parlance; we frequently hear newsreaders on television speaking of a culture of corruption in the police force, or CEOs of large corporations proclaiming the importance of their corporate culture, or politicians lamenting the state of youth culture in the outer suburbs. So the word must mean something.

In fact, in these usages the word 'culture' clearly refers to the shared beliefs or values that serve to identify a group and bind it together. Applying this interpretation to the phrase 'Australian culture' means that this concept must relate to the fundamental characteristics that are distinctive of Australian society and that connect us together as a nation. If this is so, Australian cultural policy would be a policy reflective of, expressive of, or conditioned by, these characteristics of our shared identity. As we shall see later, this does indeed summarise the sorts of issues that an Australian cultural policy might engage with.

But for now we should be aware that a more restricted interpretation of the word 'culture' also exists, one that essentially equates it with the arts. And it is in these much narrower terms, simply as arts policy, that people would tend to define cultural policy in Australia today. Indeed, if we were to trace the development of cultural policy in Australia over the last ten, twenty, fifty or a hundred years, we would surely be led to look mainly or exclusively at government treatment of the arts. So it is helpful, before we discuss the wider ramifications of cultural policy, to look at the history of arts policy from the early years to the present.

2
The history of arts policy in Australia[4]

It is often supposed that public funding of the arts in Australia is an entirely modern phenomenon. In fact, the very first recorded example of government patronage of artists in this country dates back to 1818–19, when the poet Michael Massey Robinson was granted two cows from the government herd 'for his services as Poet Laureate'. Posterity has not been kind to Mr Robinson's verse, which is now all but forgotten, but he can claim a place in history as the first ever recipient of an arts grant in Australia.[5] Indeed, not only was he the *first*, but he was also probably the *only* individual artist to receive a government grant in the nineteenth century, for it was not until the early years of the twentieth century that the first formal scheme for assisting individual artists in Australia was established. This was the Commonwealth Literary Fund, which was set up in 1908 by the Deakin Government to give financial assistance to writers. And it was not until the 1940s that consolidated and more wide-ranging programs of public support for the arts began to be contemplated in Australia; the immediate post-war years saw the establishment of the Arts Council of Australia in New South Wales, the expansion of the symphony orchestras by the ABC and in 1954 the beginnings of the Australian Elizabethan Theatre Trust.

During the 1940s, 50s and 60s the idea that government had not just a role but also a social responsibility to encourage the arts began to take root, thanks largely to the tireless efforts of Nugget Coombs, the Governor of the Commonwealth Bank, later of the Reserve Bank. Coombs never lost his determination in the face of widespread philistinism and small-mindedness amongst Prime Ministers, politicians and bureaucrats with whom he had to deal.[6] The National Theatre for which he led the crusade never quite made it into reality, but national companies in opera and ballet did, and so did the state theatre companies through his initiative which established Australia's first government-funding body, the Australian Council for the Arts, in 1967. Coombs was motivated always by the view that those who controlled the resources of a great society had an obligation to use those resources to advance the public good, and this included importantly the civilising functions of the arts. Coombs's view was shared, of course, by Gough Whitlam, and the accession of the Labor Government under Whitlam's leadership in 1972 is usually seen as marking the birth of an explicit and comprehensive, as distinct from piecemeal, arts policy at the Federal level in Australia.

It was not long after the legislation to establish the Australia Council was introduced into the Commonwealth Parliament in 1974 that the new arts policy was put to a critical test. In October of that year the Prime Minister asked the Industries Assistance Commission to enquire 'whether assistance should be accorded the performing arts in Australia and if so what should be the nature and extent of such assistance'.[7] Was it hubris that prompted Whitlam to let such a dryly economic body as the IAC loose on the arts? Was he so confident that the case for public support was beyond dispute? Certainly, Whitlam held the general view that those seeking support from the public purse had to be able to justify their claims. But in fact the real origins of the inquiry went back to the former Australian Council for the Arts, which was anxious to sort out whether commercial companies such as JC Williamson's had some claim to occasional assistance from public funds. In the event, the IAC ruffled many feathers in the arts community with questions regarded by some artists and bureaucrats as impertinent, and generally poured cold water on the way arts policy was being implemented at the time.[8] Its recommendations, not delivered until November 1976, finished up on Malcolm Fraser's desk, not Whitlam's, and were politely ignored.[9]

Indeed, in rejecting the IAC report, Fraser did so on the grounds that 'art isn't something that can be judged merely by harsh economic criteria',[10] a view that paradoxically was turned on its head during the 1980s by the very proponents of the arts who had so scorned the IAC's findings a decade before. The climate had changed. Increasingly, the cold winds of what had come to be called 'economic rationalism' were blowing through Canberra corridors, and the Government was insisting that a wide range of programs and services justify their existence in economic terms. In this way the concept of the 'arts industry' was given credibility ('bigger than beer and footwear'), allowing promotion of the arts as a significant contributor to output, employment and incomes across the nation.

In 1986 yet another inquiry, this time by a House of Representatives Standing Committee chaired by Leo McLeay, released a report that once again stirred the arts policy pot. Much attention was focussed in this report on the Australia Council, its structure and operation, and on whether its functions could be devolved partly or entirely to the States. What seemed to have been overlooked by the report's authors was the role of the individual artist, something Philip Parsons pointed out at a forum in Sydney called to discuss the enquiry's findings.[11] Then, as now, artists were doing it tough, yet somehow they managed to continue producing art while the politicians, administrators, bureaucrats, academics, journalists and the rest of the arts community argued the toss.

By now we've reached the 1990s in this brief and incomplete review of the history of government funding of the arts in Australia, and it's possible to discern certain enduring features in the matter of Commonwealth arts funding that had emerged by this time and that persist even unto the present day:

- the acceptance of a legitimate role for the Federal Government in providing assistance to the arts, whether that role is rationalised in terms of some lofty principle of the State's obligation to promote a civilised society, or whether it is based on purely economic motives—or even whether it results simply from successful political pressure exerted by an articulate and self-interested arts lobby;

- the acceptance of what can be called the 'Australian model' for arts funding, a hybrid system that includes an independent statutory arts council founded on arm's length and peer assessment principles (derived from the British model), some financial provision flowing directly from central government (as in many European countries), and some indirect support through the tax system (in emulation of the American model);

- the acceptance of a Commonwealth responsibility for major cultural institutions including the National Gallery of Australia, the National Library, the National Museum of Australia, etc. and the public broadcasting system;

- the acceptance of a secular decline in the Commonwealth's share of total arts funding as increasing levels of support are provided by State and Territory and local governments.

These four aspects of arts policy have been more or less common to both major political parties over the last twenty or thirty years, though the actual levels of funding have risen and fallen around the trend line in response to short-term political mood swings in favour of, or opposed to, the arts. Furthermore, despite overall acceptance, there have been some clear differences of emphasis between the parties within several of the policy components. For example, the Coalition has been much less committed to the idea of public broadcasting than has the ALP, a position deriving partly from the Liberal and National Parties' continuing perception of 'left-wing bias' in the ABC and partly from their ideological distaste for public-sector involvement in any area they see as being better left to private enterprise. Indeed, in recent times the Coalition under John Howard has shown itself to be quite uncomfortable with the critical and perhaps confrontational stance on sensitive issues that artists and cultural organisations can take. For example, although we have not experienced 'culture wars' to the extent seen from time to time elsewhere in the world, the Government's recent effort to control (albeit indirectly) the cultural output of the National Museum stamps it as more interventionist in these sorts of areas than any Labor government has been.[12]

Nevertheless, there is a certain sameness about the arts policies that are duly trotted out by the major parties prior to each Federal election. All the standard objectives of arts funding are there—pursuit of excellence, widening access, encouraging the expression of Australian-ness, maintaining the organisational fabric of the arts, helping individual artists. Such differences as exist can be seen in marginal adjustments to over-all levels of funding, and in a few specific programs dreamt up to capture the imagination of the public or to please the arts community—a new training facility here, a new touring program there.

But this is not the full story of the present Federal Government's arts policy. Although any political party can propose a wish-list in the run-up to an election, the government of the day actually has to implement a policy. And over the last few years the Coalition Government has introduced a new element into the arts policy-making process—policy by review. First it was the major performing arts companies that were subject to a review by a committee chaired by Helen Nugent. The Nugent report was accepted by the Minister for the Arts and most of its recommendations were put into effect. Then it was the visual arts' and the crafts' turn, with Rupert Myer's report leading to a similar policy outcome. Most recently James Strong's report on the orchestras has been released. In this case an outcry from the smaller States, whose orchestras were to be down-sized, forestalled a full adoption of its proposals.

At one level a process of policy by review is to be commended. The areas of concern were all in some sort of strife, and a sober assessment of what was needed to put it right could be seen as a sensible way to proceed. Furthermore, the various reports' recommendations of additional funds have not gone unheeded. On the other hand this is reactive rather than proactive policy-making and conveys a sense of an Arts Minister who is uninterested in the positive development of the arts, and simply waits for problems to arise before taking any action.

So there it is. Whether reactive or proactive, cultural policy in Australia has almost always been interpreted as arts policy. Yet, as noted at the outset, the notion of culture extends more widely than the arts, and (as the international examples mentioned earlier illustrate) a true cultural policy will correspondingly embrace a much wider vision than simply an arts policy. There have been one or two efforts over recent years to do just this—to stand back and look at a Federal cultural policy from a broader perspective. The most ambitious of these was the Labor Party's *Creative Nation* document of 1994.

3
Creative Nation and its legacy

The early 1990s were a time of both stability and change in Australian political life. On the one hand the community had grown accustomed to the idea of a Labor government at the Federal level; by 1994 the ALP had been in office for more than ten years, and, given the internal strife in the Coalition at the time, looked as though it could be there for ten more. On the other hand the forces of what had become known as 'globalisation' were gathering momentum in the world at large, challenging governments as never before to demonstrate that they could control and direct their nations' economic destinies and counter the impacts of cultural homogenisation in an increasingly internationalised world. These parallel circumstances—a confident government and a perception that our cultural development was under threat—prompted Prime Minister Paul Keating in July 1992 to set up a panel of eminent Australians to advise on the formulation of a Commonwealth cultural policy. The ten-member panel comprised people with experience and ideas across a range of aspects of Australian artistic and cultural life; more than half of them were practising artists.[13] The *Creative Nation* report was released in October 1994.[14] It described itself as 'the first national cultural policy in our nation's history'.

The proposals put forward in *Creative Nation* were motivated overwhelmingly by ideas about Australian identity and cultural sovereignty. The very first paragraph of the Introduction reads:

> To speak of Australian culture is to recognise our common heritage. It is to say that we share ideas, values, sentiments and traditions, and that we see in all the various manifestations of these what it means to be Australian.(p.15)

In a moment of supreme but unwitting irony, the authors of *Creative Nation* described the purpose of a cultural policy as being 'to increase the comfort [*sic*] and enjoyment of Australian life' and to 'add to our security and well-being'. (p.7) These are sentiments with which even John Howard might agree. The policy was to achieve its ends

> by shoring up our heritage in new or expanded
> national institutions and adapting technology to
> its preservation and dissemination, by creating
> new avenues for artistic and intellectual growth
> and expression and by supporting our artists and
> writers. (p.7)

By these means we would 'enable ourselves to ride the wave of global change in a way that safeguards and promotes our national culture'.

One of the most ambitious aspects of *Creative Nation* was its attempt to link cultural with economic development. It saw itself unapologetically as being not only a cultural policy, but also an economic policy. To some extent this picked up on the 1980s trend towards interpreting arts policy in economic terms to which we drew attention earlier. But it also extended these arguments much further, by embracing the cultural ramifications of new communications technologies, first through an emphasis on new media as means for cultural production, participation, dissemination and access, and second through a broader focus on cultural industry development. The essential element common to both cultural and economic progress was seen to be creativity; on the one side artists would generate innovative ideas reflecting our distinctive cultural identity, while on the other side creativity would be fostered as a key resource in the development of the new economy.

How would the Commonwealth pursue these lofty ideals? The report saw the Federal Government's role in cultural development as:

- ■ nurturing creativity and excellence;

- enabling all Australians to enjoy the widest possible range of cultural experience;
- preserving Australia's heritage;
- promoting the expression of Australia's cultural identity, including its great diversity; and
- developing lively and sustainable cultural industries, including those evolving with the emergence of new technologies.

The authors of the report proposed a variety of measures, including: an expansion of the Australia Council; a range of specific initiatives in the performing arts, the visual arts and literature; increased support for film and public broadcasting; new media development; various industry strategies; expansion of the Commonwealth's role in the protection and preservation of cultural heritage; and other programs in education and training, market development and tourism. In short, *Creative Nation* provided not only a rationale and advocacy for an active Commonwealth role in Australia's cultural development, but also a set of proposals with resources attached for putting that role into effect.

Nevertheless, it has had many detractors. Prominent among these was Donald Horne who argued (wrongly in my view) that it represented the ultimate commodification of the arts; with considerable scorn he suggested that through its characterisation of the arts as an industry, *Creative Nation* denied the fundamental *raison d'être* of artistic life.[15] Others dismissed the document as utopian and impractical, stronger on rhetoric than on substance. Certainly, the prose is occasionally vague to the point of banality:

for example, the proposition on the very first page of the Preamble that 'Democracy is the key to cultural value' is a statement of breathtaking vacuity; it might just as well have said that 'Cultural value is the key to democracy'.

Despite all the criticism, however, *Creative Nation* stands as an heroic attempt to grapple with serious problems. Furthermore, a number of its recommendations were actually implemented and some survive to this day. Yet one of the most distinctive features of the document that we noted above—its promotion of the cultural industries in the context of new information technologies—is an aspect that has largely disappeared from the Commonwealth's policy agenda. It survives in symbolic terms via a continuation of the practice, originally introduced by the Keating Government in 1994, of combining arts and communications in a single ministerial portfolio.[16] But in practical terms, the creative industries impetus has been taken up with greater enthusiasm elsewhere, not only in Australia but also overseas; it is rumoured that *Creative Nation* had some influence on the development of the 'Creative Britain' strategy of the UK government in the late 1990s.[17] Closer to home, it has been the States rather than the Commonwealth that have picked up on the creative industries agenda. Most have shown interest in industry development strategies in which new media, digital content technologies and the creative industries more generally, play a significant role, especially as components of initiatives for urban or regional growth. Perhaps this is not so surprising, given that it is somewhat easier for the States than for the Commonwealth to identify clusters of creative enterprises, or of cultural activity, as uniquely their own—as, for instance, in the promotion of their local film industries. Nevertheless, the efforts of some States to espouse progressive policies for creative industry development stand in contrast to the general lack of action at the Federal level in these areas.

The Democrats' Plan

Before leaving the matter of earlier efforts to formulate a cultural policy for Australia, we should note another salvo fired by a different political party, the Australian Democrats. In 2001 they released an 'Australian Cultural Plan' that began: 'The Australian Democrats believe Australia needs a cultural policy.' The document went on to argue that 'arts policy' was too narrow an approach to supporting culture, and proposed a series of measures to provide for the development of Australian culture on a wider front. The measures included job creation programs for artists, reform of arts education in schools, increased funding for the arts, protecting Australian culture from unfair international agreements, new provisions for cultural content in broadcasting, finance for Australian filmmaking, and importantly a suite of measures to support Indigenous cultures.[18] The Democrats may be a declining, or even a spent, force in national politics, but their determined efforts to elevate the arts and culture in the hierarchy of government priorities over many years should not be forgotten.

4
Cultural change under Howard

Two years after the publication of *Creative Nation* the social democratic government of Paul Keating was replaced by a radical conservative government led by John Howard. The brand of conservatism espoused by the Coalition could be characterised as combining a whole-hearted embrace of neo-liberal economics with an equally decisive rejection of the soft positions on social matters formerly espoused by the Liberal Party 'wets'. We have now had almost ten years of this administration. What sort of cultural change has occurred under Howard? More particularly, to what extent has the Prime Minister put his own stamp on Australia's cultural development?

As Paul Kelly has observed,[19] John Howard exhibits a paradoxical mixture of forward-looking and backward-looking attitudes in his vision of the sort of society Australia should be and the direction in which we should be heading: he is simultaneously an economic liberal and a cultural traditionalist. On the economy Howard is an uncompromising advocate of hard-line free-market reform. He aspires to lead Australia towards an economic utopia where deregulation, privatisation and the dominance of the private sector are absolute; indeed, he could be described as more Thatcherite than Thatcher. In cultural terms, however, his vision looks back to the past for its in-spiration. His description of Australian life as 'relaxed and comfortable'[20] is based on a nostalgic evocation of a peaceful suburbia, of inherited Britishness, of a world where the values of Don Bradman were the glue that held the community together. The symbols of nation-hood to which the Prime Minister constantly refers are drawn from what he sees as defining moments in our history—Gallipoli, Kokoda—opportunities for the Australian battler to emerge as hero and for the pivotal characteristic of mateship to be forged. Yet there is a paradox here too: at the same time as Howard enunciates his view of what characterises Australian-ness, and celebrates the patriotic spirit at events like the opening of the 2000 Olympic Games in Sydney, he declares that 'as a nation we're over all that identity stuff'—no need to go on about it, we know who we are.[21]

Howard's backward-looking cultural vision does not seem to embrace the arts in any significant way, although if the cultural ambit is extended, as it should be, to include popular forms such as sport, a different picture emerges; his passion for sport is strong indeed, especially in his incarnation as a self-confessed 'cricket tragic'. But when it comes to the theatre or music or the visual arts, he seems to have no particular personal commitment. His biographers do not record any artis-tic activities or interests in his background,[22] and he is rarely, if ever, seen at arts events; his wife and children attend without him. No doubt his traditional cultural tastes would be sympathetic towards such mainstream cultural institutions as the nation's public museums and galleries, but it may reasonably be surmised that he neither knows of, nor cares about, contemporary art in any of its manifestations. It follows that the role of art as a medium for social criticism, or of artists as social critics, is not one that he would be likely to recognise, let alone endorse.

So much for the outward and visible signs of Howard's cultural position. There's also a more subtle indicator of the cultural directions in which Australia is moving under the present Federal Government. A number of different areas of government policy-making are built upon certain cultural values which are not explicit, but which may be inferred from the nature of the policy measures that the government pursues. Let us look briefly at four areas—economic policy, immigration, Indigenous affairs, and Australian independence—and ask what the cultural underpinnings of policy in each area tell us and whether the values they represent may be regarded as broadly reflective of Australian attitudes.[23]

First, the last ten years have witnessed considerable hardening of economic policy, with consequent effects on the way in which the average Australian perceives the world. We are constantly persuaded that we need more material goods, and when we can't afford them, an obliging bank will only too happily lend us the money. Economic jargon has permeated our lives: when we travel by aeroplane we are no longer passengers but customers, and universities don't have students, they have clients. Once-great public institutions are now profit-maximising corporations. When we go to see a play we are not members of the audience, but consumers providing financial input to the theatre company's bottom line. There has been inexorable movement in Australia, as in a number of other Western countries, from the public to the private, from the collective to the individual, from concerns about equity and fairness to an obsession with efficiency, from businesses that serve their customers to corporations that serve their shareholders. The objectives of government economic and social policy reflect and encourage these trends; public policy in areas such as education, health and welfare is increasingly framed in economic terms—efficiency benchmarks, service delivery, key performance indicators, contractual obligations. In these circumstances, if people have deeper aspirations for the kind of society in which they live, these are simply assumed to be subservient to dominant economic goals.

Of course, in giving supremacy to economic growth as a national objective for this country, Howard's economic agenda is little different from that of the Keating and Hawke governments before him. Furthermore, the economic prosperity that Australia has enjoyed in the recent past seems to have paid electoral dividends for the Government and, indeed, there is evidence that Australians take pride in the country's economic achievements.[24] However, whether the values of individualism and materialism that underpin the liberal economic project accord with the Australian ethos of mateship and concern for others is another matter. Several social commentators have pointed to increasing disillusion with material rewards as a source of well-being and happiness,[25] and the cultural value of trust in key players in the economic system seems to be in decline; for example, although trust in Australia's public institutions remains reasonably constant, there has been a substantial erosion of trust in major corporations over the last ten years.[26] Furthermore, there are signs that people do not want to see deregulation and privatisation pushed as far as Howard would like; for example, there is still a majority opposed to the full privatisation of Telstra.

Second, immigration presents a confusing picture. Despite appearances to the contrary, the empirical evidence suggests that Australians on the whole now have a more positive attitude towards immigration than they did ten years ago and that they are no less tolerant of refugees.[27] In particular, a majority in the community recognise that the immigration of people from widely disparate cultural traditions has been beneficial to the good health of Australian cultural life. If this is true, it suggests that government policy and pronouncements in this area have been out of step with the popular mood, because, although Howard has talked up the benefits of immigration, particularly of skilled labour, he has also demonised refugees. Yet, while border control may meet with general approval, there is serious doubt as to whether the treatment of refugees in detention accords with traditional Australian values of tolerance, fair play and respect for human rights. The recent softening of the Government's position in this regard is no more than a minor shift in an overall policy stance that seems markedly out of alignment with Australian cultural attitudes as traditionally conceived.

Third, Howard's refusal to apologise to Indigenous Australians for past wrongs, and the stalling of the reconciliation process, mark a significant cultural reversal that has occurred since 1996. While expressing concern about the appalling state of Indigenous health, education and welfare, Howard has shown little understanding of fundamental issues affecting the relationship between European and Aboriginal society—the importance of land rights, the significance of an apology, the centrality of Indigenous culture, Aboriginal people's need for respect rather than condescension. The sentiments expressed in Keating's celebrated Redfern speech of December 1992, or in the dignified and heartfelt apology written on John Howard's behalf by John Clarke and delivered by the PM's actor namesake in the run-up to the 2000 Olympic Games,[28] are not likely to be shared by the man himself. In these respects again, we might see some disjunction between Howard's views and those of a majority of the Australian people.

Finally, there can be few issues that exemplify Howard's cultural stance more clearly than that of the republic. In 1999 he effectively scuttled what had seemed like inexorable progress towards a republic, and in the six years since he has made no effort to bring the issue back into the public debate. Furthermore, in the wider area of Australian independence and self-determination, he has moved much closer than his predecessors towards aligning Australia's foreign policy interests with those of the United States, to the point where he was willing to commit this country to war in Iraq when a clear majority of the population was opposed to such action. Again, it is not evident whether Howard's treatment of the republic issue, or his willingness to bend Australia's traditionally independent stance in foreign policy to the wishes of the United States, are reflective of what he actually believes to be the true will of the people, or (as seems more probable) an effort to impose a different set of values and to take the country along a different cultural pathway.

Where does all this lead us in thinking about a cultural policy? I have argued that we have seen quite a lot of cultural change in the last ten years, some of it brought about by long-term demographic and social trends beyond anyone's control, but some of it managed or encouraged by the Federal Government as led by the Prime Minister. It has brought us to a point where it would seem to be in the national interest to take stock of where we are and where we are going. Are we, as David Williamson has suggested, a cruise ship 'all alone in the south seas sailing to God knows where'?[29] Or are we satisfied with who we are and how our Federal Government represents us to ourselves and to the world? Asking these questions right now is particularly timely in view of recent international developments that have encouraged countries to think carefully about their cultural policies. These stimuli arise from no less a body than the United Nations, via its cultural organisation UNESCO, which has been giving a lot of time to thinking about cultural diversity.

5

An international framework for a national cultural policy

Towards the end of September 2001, a week or so after 9/11, the General Conference of UNESCO sat down to consider a *Universal Declaration on Cultural Diversity.*[30] In doing so they focused world-wide attention on the importance of culture as an expression of fundamental human values. In its recognition of the plurality of human civilisation, the *Universal Declaration* raised critical questions about the nature of the societies in which we live, and about how we live together. Most importantly for our present discussion, it elevated the role that cultural policy can and should play in national and international affairs.

What sort of cultural diversity did the UNESCO member states endorse? The twelve articles of the *Declaration* encompass identity, human rights, creativity and international solidarity. Together they comprise a comprehensive account of how far the notion of cultural diversity can be taken to extend in contemporary international discourse. According to this document, cultural diversity may be defined in the following terms.

1   Diversity is seen as being embodied in the 'uniqueness and plurality' of the identities of various societies and groups, a common heritage of humankind. Since culture itself is intrinsic to the realisation of human aspirations, it is argued that cultural diversity will be an important factor in promoting economic, social and cultural development in both industrialised and developing countries.

2   Promotion of cultural diversity can take place only in accordance with respect for fundamental human rights. No one should invoke cultural diversity in order to defend, for example, 'traditional' cultural practices that deny basic rights and freedoms, such as those of women or of minorities.

3   The distinctive nature of cultural goods and services such as movies, artworks, television programs, music recordings, and so forth must be recognised. Apart from being commercial commodities, these goods have an important role as purveyors of cultural messages. Since cultural goods and services arise from human creativity, it follows that cultural diversity will be enhanced in conditions conducive to creative activity and to the production and distribution of a wide range of cultural product.

4   Finally, the UNESCO member states declared that to enable the benefits arising from cultural diversity to have effect worldwide, international co-operation and dialogue will be required involving public institutions, the private sector and civil society.

Following on from the adoption of the *Declaration*, UNESCO set in train a process aimed at formulating a treaty or convention on cultural diversity to which countries would be able to sign up if they supported its provisions. In fact, the treaty, as it has evolved, is more accurately labelled a *cultural policy* convention, its practical effect being to encourage member states to look to their cultural policies and to raise the profile of culture on their respective policy agendas.

In moving towards a cultural convention, UNESCO was responding to a number of different pressures. Three stand out most noticeably. First, there has been the problem of cultural goods in international trade—a matter of special concern to Australia, given the imbroglio over the treatment of cultural goods in negotiations for the recent US/Australia Free Trade Agreement. For many years the organisations regulating world trade—first the General Agreement on Tariffs and Trade (the GATT) and now the World Trade Organisation (the WTO)—have had difficulty dealing with cultural goods, especially film, television programs and other audiovisual products. Proponents of free trade have said that cultural goods are nothing special and should be treated like any other merchandise. Countries like France and Canada, however, have resisted this view and have won the right for a 'cultural exception' to apply to such products. This means that these countries can continue to protect their local cultural industries against the market power of major exporters of cultural goods, in particular the United States. Other people, however, have suggested, that cultural goods should not be handled via the WTO, but accorded separate trading arrangements, and that a cultural diversity convention would be an appropriate forum in which to develop and establish these.

The second impetus towards a treaty has come from the perception that globalisation is increasingly threatening people's sense of their own cultural identity. There is no doubt that this fear has been an important factor in mobilising 'anti-globalisation' protests around the world, where banners often proclaim the United States or transnational corporations as villains seeking to impose a homogenised culture on everything and everyone. In such demonstrations diverse targets and problems are often conflated and their purposes blurred. Nevertheless, there is no denying the depth of apprehension amongst the participants about where the world seems to be heading. These are significant fears and they have done much to encourage the idea of a convention for the protection of cultural diversity. Such an instrument, it is argued, could at least help us to distinguish the positive and negative impacts of globalisation, fostering the former while keeping the latter at bay.

Finally, a strong impetus towards a cultural diversity treaty has stemmed from a profound sense that countries of the Third World are losing out in the process of economic and cultural development. Cultural exports from developing countries are swallowed up in the global marketplace, while at the same time these countries have few resources to protect and promote their own cultural expressions. A treaty may provide them with a policy framework for pursuit of culturally sustainable development.

What has happened? After a lengthy process of drafting and redrafting, involving countless committees and endless negotiation, in 2005 a form of words was finally agreed to for a 'Preliminary Draft Convention on the Protection and Promotion of the Diversity of Cultural Expressions', to give it its full and rather cumbersome title. The treaty affirms the rights of countries to formulate cultural policies to foster creative expression and to promote the positive aspects of cultural diversity within a context of respect for fundamental human rights and freedoms. The convention pays particular attention to the need for sustainable cultural and economic development, and proposes mechanisms for international cooperation and solidarity. It deals with threats to cultural diversity, however they might arise, by encouraging countries to take protective action if vulnerable forms of cultural expression are seen to be in danger of extinction or serious curtailment.

Throughout the negotiation process the United States, a country that has only recently returned to the UNESCO family, vigorously opposed any effort to limit the free access of cultural product to any of the world's markets. In practice, of course, this opposition was directed at the 'cultural exception' concept and at policies such as local content quotas that protect domestic film and television industries from being overwhelmed by competition from Hollywood. But countries on the receiving end of American cultural exports were unimpressed by the free-trade arguments; they pointed out that 85 percent of movie tickets sold worldwide were for Hollywood films, whereas only one percent of movies shown in the US were from other countries. Artists and producers of audio-visual material in both developed and developing countries find it virtually impossible to make their voices heard unless there is some form of protection or assistance from government. Moreover, many believe that America has no right to take the moral high ground on protectionism—just ask any agricultural exporter.

Australia's interests

What are Australia's interests in the areas covered by the draft convention? We are a culturally diverse nation with a long tradition of cultural support and engagement. Our various forms of cultural expression are distinctive and strong, and vital to our cultural development. But they are indeed vulnerable in the modern world, and we would benefit from a clearer recognition in trading arrangements of the special characteristics of cultural goods. Any moves to strengthen processes of cultural policy formulation, to promote intercultural dialogue and to render assistance in cultural development to poorer countries, would seem to deserve our unequivocal support. But no. When it came to a vote for adoption of the draft treaty at the UNESCO General Conference meeting in Paris on 20 October 2005, Australia abstained. Of the 154 countries represented at this historic meeting, 148 voted in favour of the convention, America (not surprisingly) and Israel voted against, and there were three other abstentions: Honduras, Liberia and Nicaragua.

Why did we take such a conspicuously oppositional stand in an international arena where the diplomatic implications of voting behaviour do not go unnoticed? It is tempting to read Australia's abstention as simply another gesture of support for our great and powerful ally, and indeed this is exactly how it is being interpreted by many observers both here and abroad. The official explanation, however, is based on technicalities, including concern that some aspects of the convention might conflict with some of our domestic policies or with our obligations under other international treaties to which we are a signatory. But these are scarcely credible grounds—most other countries are in exactly the same position. Indeed, government after government lined up to say that their positive vote was based on an assumption that their other domestic and international obligations would not be compromised. New Zealand, for example, said that it assumed the provision promoting international movements of artists would not conflict with their own migration laws.

In one sense Australia does have a case: there are some flaws and inconsistencies in the document that are going to have to be dealt with in the times ahead. However, many countries pointed to these problems, yet still managed to vote in favour. They understood, as apparently we did not, that voting for adoption of the convention at this stage was really just an expression of agreement with its broad principles; formal adherence to its provisions applied only to those countries that would eventually ratify the treaty in a couple of years' time (a minimum of 30 are needed). For now, the great majority of the world's nations have realised the symbolic importance of showing support for artistic and cultural values in an uncertain and divided world. The fact that we are not among them gives us a prominence on the world stage that can hardly be in Australia's interests. Indeed our new-found image as a cultural pariah should be a matter of considerable worry to anyone who is interested in Australia's cultural standing in the world at large and concerned about the prospects for our future cultural development at home.

6
Towards a new cultural accord

At last we come to the crunch: what is the answer to the question posed by the title of this essay? Do we need a national-level cultural policy? Economists have a reputation for being equivocal; they are forever saying 'on the one hand this, on the other hand that', or 'it depends', or 'other things being equal' etc. etc. I am an economist, so it should come as no surprise if my answer to the question is 'Yes and no'. Or rather 'No and yes'. I would answer 'No' to the sort of magisterial cultural statement handed down by the Prime Minister, the Cabinet or a parliamentary committee; and 'No' to the proposition that a cultural policy should consist of a single document or a single piece of legislation; but 'Yes' to a much more exciting and wide-ranging proposition—the opening up of a broad-ranging discussion about the role of the arts and culture in our society, and the forging of a new cultural accord between government and people. Cultural policy is not a single definable thing, but a pervasive mixture that not only determines the immediate and obvious ways in which we practise our culture—through the arts, for example—but also affects a broader range of economic and social policies that have undeniable cultural content. By spelling out how the different aspects of cultural policy fit into an overall policy agenda, we can raise the profile of culture in national affairs and provide a clearer direction for policy-making that is consistent with the sort of Australian society that we want to inhabit.

What would be the ambit of such a broad-ranging cultural policy discussion? Four different policy areas can be distinguished that, taken together, make up an overall framework for cultural policy. These are: the 'core' areas of arts and heritage policy; cultural and economic policy; cultural and social policy; and cultural and foreign policy. In each of these areas there is a wide range of specific policy applications where cultural considerations may be relevant. In the following paragraphs I discuss some representative cases in each area, defining more clearly what needs to be done.

(i) The creative 'core': arts and heritage policy

At the very heart of any cultural policy are the various ways in which government supports the country's imaginative and creative life. This life is expressed through the production and consumption of art in all its forms, and through other ways in which we think about who we are, in particular by engaging with our movable and immovable cultural heritage. So we can define the 'core' of a cultural policy as comprising, at the very least, arts and heritage policy.

Looking first at the arts, our earlier discussion highlighted some of the problems with the current government's arts policy, including its tendency to be reactive rather than proactive, to be steady-as-she-goes rather than expansionary, and tending to suppress rather than foster the arts' role as social critic. Although current levels of support from the Commonwealth for the arts are by no means insignificant in per capita terms, it is becoming apparent that they are insufficient to guarantee a sustainable arts sector, measured in either quantitative or qualitative terms. The Government's own reports on the financial circumstances of performing companies and of other areas of the arts, as well as research highlighting the meagre financial rewards to artistic labour,[31] indicate that the future is bleak without more money, and that there is a lot of creative potential in the arts that could be unlocked if only more funding were available. It is worth remembering that the case for supporting the arts in a free-market economy such as ours does not have to be seen as special pleading, nor as rent-seeking by a favoured cultural elite. On the contrary, there is ample evidence that the arts give rise to generalised community benefits that are valued even by those who do not consume the arts directly themselves. For example, as long ago as the early 1980s Glenn

Withers and I demonstrated that Australian taxpayers recognised these benefits and were willing to see their taxes spent on producing them.[32] I have no doubt that, although dollar amounts may vary, a similar result would be found, were we to repeat the survey today. Even the driest economist will concede that when markets fail, as they do in their failure to provide the public-good benefits of the arts, a presumptive case exists for collective action to remedy the problem, in this case most immediately via government subsidy.

It is not only these public-good benefits of the arts that are important in making an economic case for support. There are also other economic and social effects that may be the focus of government policy, including the arts' contribution to employment creation, wealth generation, urban revitalisation, social cohesion, and so on. But, although the economic case may be strong, there is a danger that it may become the only basis on which governments intervene, conveying a sense that the health of the arts is reflected solely in their financial performance. So, for example, publicly-supported theatre companies, orchestras, dance ensembles, art galleries etc. may feel that funding authorities look to economic sustainability rather than cultural vitality, as a basis for continued funding.

In the international arena these concerns have led to a debate about how to introduce cultural value alongside economic value into the making of public policy towards the arts and culture. In the United Kingdom, for example, government obsession with laying down performance targets for cultural organisations is argued to have subverted the organisations' cultural purpose; the measurable economic and social benefits that they provide have become more important to policy-making than the artistic or cultural activity itself.[33] In the United States, a recent report by the RAND Corporation on reframing the debate in America about the benefits of the arts[34] discusses the wide range of economic and social benefits that the arts bring to individuals and to communities, but calls the intrinsic value of the arts 'the missing link'. This report argues that the intrinsic benefits of the arts have become marginalised in public discourse, in part because they are difficult to measure. Both of these influential reports call for a new approach to public policy formulation with respect to the arts and culture, one that makes explicit the full range of value created by these activities. It is important that this debate be carried forward here in Australia.

The same arguments are relevant to the other 'core' component of cultural policy—government assistance to the protection, restoration and management of cultural heritage. Policy towards movable heritage (collections of artworks, archives, artefacts, other items held by museums, and so on) is currently undergoing a long-overdue process of rationalisation via the newly-established Collections Council of Australia. In regard to immovable heritage (mainly historic buildings and sites), an inquiry by the Productivity Commission is under way to look at the justification for government support for the preservation and management of Australia's historic built heritage, and to make recommendations for improvements to policy. Some observers have feared that the Commission's reputation for applying rigorous economics to everything that comes under its scrutiny might signal an end to government involvement in this area. In fact, the Inquiry's Discussion Paper indicates very clearly a willingness by the Commissioners to entertain the proposition that heritage is, like the arts, an area where market failure occurs. Although heritage markets can deliver some direct-use benefits, the overwhelming source of real and measurable benefit lies outside the market; this benefit derives particularly from the general contribution of heritage to the understanding and expression of Australian identity. In addition, the intrinsic value of heritage in its own right—its essential cultural value—can provide a parallel justification for government policy, just as in the case of the arts.

Having outlined the basis on which these core cultural policies can be rationalised, we can now consider the administrative mechanisms by which they can be delivered. With regard to the arts, the role and functions of the Australia Council seem to be a constant topic of debate,[35] notwithstanding the relatively small proportion of overall cultural funding at the Commonwealth level that is channelled through the Council. Several opportunities have been missed in recent years for a constructive re-think and expansion of the Australia Council's role, with the result that the Council sometimes gives the impression that it just wants to keep its head down and defend its territory. A re-thinking of arts policy at the Federal level could look to ways in which the Australia Council might expand its activities into new and imaginative programs and responsibilities, as a means of improving the artistic and cultural life of this country. In the case of heritage, the functions of the Collections Council of Australia and the Australian Heritage Council are critical; given the overlapping jurisdictions with which both bodies deal, the forging of co-operative arrangements with State/Territory and local governments are an essential aspect of policy delivery.

(ii) Cultural and economic policy

Two of the most important areas of government interest where cultural and economic policies intersect are those that relate to the cultural industries and the media. While it may not be easy to give clear definition to the term 'cultural industries', conventionally they include film and television production, publishing, video and computer games, and so on. As was noted earlier, the Commonwealth Government has largely left industry policy in these areas to the States, although there is still an important Federal involvement in film financing.

The growth of the cultural industries is closely linked to the structural transformations that have been occurring in most developed economies over the last few decades. These changes have involved a transition from a manufacturing to a service economy, and from there, as a result of technological advances in communications and information processing, into what some observers call the information or the knowledge economy. Strategic competitive advantage in this new commercial environment is supposed to lie with those firms that can maintain a creative edge. In these circumstances the cultural industries exist not simply to produce cultural goods and services, but also to act as a generator and supplier of creativity, that elusive but vital resource that brings economic success in the contemporary world.[36] Governments, so the rhetoric goes, can enhance national competitiveness by industry policies aimed at fostering the creative industries through targeted assistance measures of various sorts, including investment allowances, tax concessions, subsidies and much more.

A fair amount of hype surrounds these claims— there is, after all, nothing particularly new about the so-called 'new economy', and most of our wealth is still created by traditional agricultural, manufacturing and service industries. Nonetheless, the significance of the cultural industries themselves, and their products, is undeniable, and it is important to understand where they fit in a broader cultural policy framework. If cultural policy is about ensuring that cultural value creation is recognised alongside the generation of economic value, a combined cultural and economic policy should focus on the content-creation aspects of these industries. This has relevance for Australia insofar as we are much more likely in the future to succeed as content providers for the new communications technologies than as producers of the technologies themselves. In turn, it is essential to realise that creative content arises from the primary forms of creative expression, namely the production of sound, image and text, in other words from the core creative arts. If this is so, it follows that one of the most enduring foundations upon which the cultural industries can be built will be a flourishing arts sector. By this means we can connect the industry-development aspects of economic and cultural policy back to the fundamental matter of support for the creative arts.

In this regard we should mention the film industry, which occupies an ambivalent position between being a core component of the creative arts on the one hand, and a multi-million dollar commercial industry on the other. This ambivalence is reflected in government policy-making towards the industry: should support be provided only for projects with a strong chance of commercial success, or should specific criteria of artistic and cultural merit be applied? Of course, everybody looks for projects that have both, but everybody knows that few projects do. Meanwhile there are on-going questions about how policy could be improved. More money is the self-evident first step. However, if the Federal Government did indeed want to give the industry a boost, an issue would arise as to which of the Commonwealth agencies would make best use of additional funds: the Australian Film Commission, the Film Finance Corporation, and/or the smaller production organisations Film Australia or SBS Independent? The policy mix is also important: for example, could private sector participation be cranked up a little via some marginal improvements to tax concessions for film investors? Might the short-lived Commercial Television Production Fund be revived? What is the right balance between direct (subsidy/grants) and indirect (tax-based) support for the industry? Given the interconnections between the industry and other parts of the cultural sector (e.g. as an employer of actors), how can co-ordination of cultural policy in different fields be improved?

The other area that I can use to illustrate where cultural policy and economic policy intersect is that of government regulation of the media. Almost exclusively these days government decisions concerning media regulation are guided by commercial rather than cultural criteria. Yet there are clear cultural ramifications arising from changes to cross-media ownership rules, the introduction of new technologies, the sale of spectrum, and so on. Even more directly, local content regulations have a major impact both on the production of Australian material and on the types of cultural messages to which the population has access. If cultural policy is to be comprehensive at the national level, it is essential that media policy as it affects the commercial sector be re-articulated to account explicitly for the cultural impact of economically-driven decisions.

Of course, the other aspect of the Government's media policy is its attitude to the public broadcasters, a matter touched on earlier. Suffice it to say here that an independent, high-quality, publicly-funded broadcasting system has proved to be an essential element in defining and enhancing the cultural life of this country. The charters of the ABC and SBS stand as a clear affirmation of their role in this respect, and endorsement of them would be expected to form an integral part of any expression of government cultural policy toward the public broadcasting sector. But noble sentiments are not enough on their own, they must be backed up by sufficient resources to enable the broadcasters to do their job effectively. Furthermore, the broadcasters' own policy-making must be constantly directed toward fulfilling their charter obligations; in this respect the decline over the last few years in the ABC's output of Australian drama can be seen as a policy failure as much as a result of lack of resources.[37]

(iii) Cultural and social policy

Two areas where cultural policy intersects with social policy are the treatment of refugees, and Indigenous affairs. Since both of these have already been discussed, it only remains to say that the purpose of invoking cultural policy in these areas is to make explicit the cultural assumptions and values on which present government policy is based. In the case of refugees this means not simply raising questions surrounding human rights as fundamental values in defining Australian culture, but also extending the debate to embrace our attitudes to cultural difference, and the role cultural diversity plays in contemporary Australian society at a time when multiculturalism, however it is interpreted, faces an uncertain future. In regard to the treatment of Indigenous Australians, there can be few areas of social policy where the need for cultural understanding is more important in the policy development process. Informed public discussion of these issues cannot fail to bring to light a range of cultural shortcomings in the way in which present Indigenous policy is formed and implemented, and must point the way towards a more enlightened exercise of government responsibilities in this area.

(iv) Cultural and foreign policy

The final area in which a more clearly-defined cultural policy is needed is that of Australia's foreign relations. At one level there is a direct engagement here, namely in the area of international cultural exchange. It is well known that one of the most effective ways in which the image of a country and its people can be enhanced is through cultural programs that show off the country's arts and culture elsewhere in the world. Not only are cultural exchanges mutually beneficial in promoting understanding and goodwill, but there may also be economic payoffs—the old maxim, that 'where culture leads, trade follows', still holds true. Although we already do a lot in this respect, we could do a lot more. Countries such as Britain, France and Germany have, through the British Council, Alliance Française and the Goethe Institut respectively, advanced their national interests in a variety of tangible and intangible ways. A re-thinking of Australian cultural policy at the international level could well finally grasp the nettle of establishing such an organisation to represent Australian interests abroad, especially in the Asia-Pacific region, where our economic and cultural relationships are of the utmost importance.

At a more general level is the question of the extent to which Australia's foreign policy reflects the sort of cultural values we regard as important. For instance, as mentioned earlier, many in the community are disturbed by the close alignment of Australian foreign policy with that of the United States, and it has been strongly suggested that a distinctive and independent Australian culture is somehow being made subservient to American cultural values in this process. Closer to home is the image of Australia in the Pacific Region. Interventions in peace-building processes in the Solomon Islands or in maintaining law and order in Papua New Guinea have achieved some success, yet it remains unclear whether the cultural impacts of these initiatives have been either understood or welcomed. Again, informed debate about the cultural underpinnings of policy in these sorts of areas should be made an integral part of the more general policy-making process.

7
Conclusions: the way ahead

Let me try to draw together the threads of this essay. My reasons for asking the question that constitutes my title stem from a perception that we stand at a critical point in our development as a nation. There is a sense in the air that as a society we are economically wealthy but culturally impoverished, or else, if not quite impoverished, at least uncertain about what our cultural values are and in what direction they may be changing. In the specific world of the arts there is a sense of unease; at one level we see a lot of participation in the performing arts, in the visual arts, in reading and writing books, yet at the same time many of our cultural organisations are starved for funds, creative artists are out of work, and a great deal of valuable artistic work is simply not being seen or heard.

Of course, there's no point in blaming government for this state of affairs, always assuming, that is, that these misgivings have substance. In regard to the arts, for example, we can't say that government at whatever level can be held responsible for the state of the world. The arts exist in their own right as a self-determining system of human thought and action. The pattern of artistic activity at any given time depends on how much and what sort of art people demand, and how much and what sort of art artists are impelled to create. In the past we have seen the arts flourish as a result of demand from a patron or public sufficiently enlightened to call forth great art, and we have also seen how the creativity, hard work and occasional genius of artists will go on producing art whatever the circumstances. Similarly, at the wider level there's no use holding governments responsible for who we are or who we think we are. We get the sort of society we make for ourselves and it's our own cultural perceptions and aspirations that shape our destiny, not those of any government.

So, why express these vaguely-felt anxieties by suggesting a possible need for a cultural policy? The reason is that governments do in fact affect what's happening and what can happen, for the simple reason that in a democratic polity they represent the collective will of all of us, they are the guardians of the public interest, and they have the coercive power to take our money and use it for good purposes that are beyond what we as individuals can do on our own. This in the broadest sense is what is meant by policy—not a specific measure or set of measures, but a more general expression of how governments discharge the trust we place in them.

Thus, a cultural policy is not a single document or statement or piece of legislation, it is the collection of actions that governments take to create the conditions under which our cultural values, and indeed our whole cultural life, can find their expression. I have suggested that at the present moment in Australia's development we need a re-evaluation of what constitutes our cultural policy in this broad all-embracing sense. I have drawn attention to some of the conflicting messages that bring about this need:

- the Federal Government pledges its support for the arts, but is reluctant to provide the levels of funding that could catalyse a new renaissance in the production and consumption of the arts across Australia;
- the Prime Minister asserts that there is no need to discuss Australian identity, yet beats the patriotic drum;
- we see ourselves as a tolerant fair-minded people, yet treat refugees in detention in ways that are completely contrary to these basic cultural values;
- we recognise that Indigenous Australians are amongst the most disadvantaged in our society, yet we continue to show cultural insensitivity in trying to remedy the situation;

- we see ourselves as an independent country with distinctive cultural attributes, yet we seem to have shelved any discussion of how we can better reflect that independence in our constitutional arrangements; and
- we profess the virtues of intercultural dialogue and mutual understanding between nations, yet we abstain from supporting an international cultural convention aimed at achieving these very objectives.

So, I am arguing that we need a process by which to re-examine the directions of our cultural development: how can our core commitments to supporting the arts be better discharged and how can we explore more openly the cultural foundations of our economic, social and foreign policy? There are a number of ways in which we could proceed. They could be described as top-down or bottom-up.

The most obvious top-down process is to get together a group of people covering a range of interests, expertise and representation across the social and cultural spectrum and ask them to sit around a table for as long as it takes and come up with a document that can be put out for public discussion. This was essentially the approach used for *Creative Nation*. The advantage of this process is seen in the focus it provides for a discussion on cultural policy, but the obvious disadvantage of it is that, however well-meaning the committee members, it is a process that smacks of a cultural elite telling us what to do. In any case, the likelihood of anything like *Creative Nation* being sanctioned by the present Federal Government is remote, to say the least. Nonetheless, some effort to gather together a cultural statement of some sort as a basis for discussion could be contemplated, whether put together by politicians, bureaucrats, groups of experts, groups of non-experts, or anyone else.

However, a more sensible as well as more realistic way to proceed would be to look towards a bottom-up approach, whereby grass-roots individuals, communities and other groups might coalesce around particular issues to bring forth discussion papers, manifestos, draft policy statements or whatever, to open up debate on particular elements in the cultural policy mosaic. At some point a cultural 'summit' could even be proposed, at which these interests were brought together for informed discussion of the issues in a way that would heighten public awareness and contribute to the policy- development process.

At heart, I suppose, the territory that I have been traversing in this essay does indeed come down to a reflection on Australian identity. Despite John Howard's assertion that we don't need to discuss this notion any longer, there are many aspects of Australian culture that would repay a critical examination. Identity is something that affects us all. Nicholas Jose, talking about his writing, said recently that he was concerned about identity because he was 'interested [...] in what lies behind what we see',[38] and it is the subterranean aspects of our culture as much as its outward manifestations that we might think about under the broad rubric of a cultural policy.

Whatever approach to pursuing these ideas is adopted—and the various possibilities are by no means mutually exclusive—the desired result would be to foster public debate about the state of the arts and culture in Australia at a critical stage in our national development. Such a debate might well help to alleviate some of the uncertainties and anxieties mentioned in these pages, and could not but re-invigorate our artistic and cultural growth.

Epilogue

Throughout the history of the arts, one of the most powerful ways in which art has discharged its function as social critic has been through satire. This is particularly true of the Australian theatre, which has a long satirical tradition of writers and performers who have gently, and often not so gently, satirised aspects of the Australian condition. So, given the subject matter of this essay, it is appropriate to end it on a satirical note. Thinking about Australian identity in the contemporary world, I am drawn to the words of Bob Ellis, who has written much that bears directly or indirectly on this matter. But on this occasion I want to quote not Ellis himself, but his *alter ego* Max Gillies, delivering words written by Guy Rundle in *Your Dreaming: the Prime Minister's Cultural Convention*, a show that was first performed in May 2001 at Melbourne's Playbox under the direction of Aubrey Mellor and subsequently seen nationally. Here Ellis/Gillies/Rundle reflects on the state of the nation:

> A land not chosen by the people, a people not chosen by the land, a people with no choice but to make of it what they will and to reconcile and be reconciled and take a gamble on the lucky country and try to work out if any of it meant anything, and if we have any special reason to be here, if we are the carriers of the flame or whether it was all just cricket and the beach and other people's television, or whether there is anything we have to teach the world, any new way to cut the Gordian knot and to solve the Sphinx's riddle and to tend the Delphic flame … and come to our bounty and inherit the kingdom of somethingness to take power in the vernacular republic and to pass the torch on to future generations … so that in our age the light on the hill will burn afresh and not gutter and die![39]

As has been observed many times, art often surpasses reality.

Endnotes

1   (London: Faber and Faber, 1983), p.25.

2   These examples are drawn from documents prepared by the Council of Europe and ERICarts under the general title *Cultural Policies in Europe: a Compendium of Basic Facts and Trends* (Strasbourg: Council of Europe, 2002).

3   Robert Borofsky, 'Cultural possibilities', in UNESCO World Culture Report (1998), p.64.

4   For further detail and statistical tabulations, see David Throsby, 'Public funding of the arts in Australia—1900 to 2000', *Yearbook of Australia 2001* (Canberra: Australian Bureau of Statistics, 2001), pp.548–61.

5   See further in the article on Robinson in *The Australian Encyclopaedia* (Sydney: Australian Geographic, 1996), pp.2599–2600.

6   See Coombs' autobiography, *Trial Balance* (Melbourne: Macmillan, 1981), pp.217–59.

7   *Industries Assistance Commission, Report on Assistance to the Performing Arts* (Canberra: Australian Government Publishing Service, 1976), p.137.

8   See Gough Whitlam, *The Whitlam Government 1972–1975* (Ringwood: Penguin, 1985), p.564.

9   J.C. Williamson's subsequently went into liquidation.

10 Quoted by Tim Rowse, *Arguing the Arts: the Funding of the Arts in Australia* (Ringwood: Penguin, 1985),

p.34. Fraser's speech in the House of Representatives is also quoted (at greater length) by Justin Macdonnell in *Arts Minister? Government Policy and the Arts* (Sydney: Currency Press, 1992), p.204, in his detailed account of the IAC Report and its aftermath.

11   See Shooting the Pianist: the Role of Government in the Arts , ed. Philip Parsons (Sydney: Currency Press, 1987), pp.9–20.

12   David Marr has drawn attention to several similar examples from the theatre; see his Philip Parsons Memorial Lecture 'Theatre under Howard', Sydney, 9 October 2005.

13   The members as at February 1993 were Gillian Armstrong, Thea Astley, Rodney Hall, Jennifer Kee, Jill Kitson, Michael Leslie, Graeme Murphy, Bruce Petty, Leo Schofield and Peter Spearritt.

14   Commonwealth of Australia, *Creative Nation: Commonwealth Cultural Policy* (Canberra: Department of Communications and the Arts, 1994).

15   See *Looking at Leadership: Australia in the Howard Years* (Ringwood: Viking, 2001), pp.139–40.

16   There is also a Digital Content Strategy introduced by the Australian Government in 2001, and a recent initiative within the Prime Minister's Science, Engineering and Innovation Council to consider the role of creativity in the 'innovation economy', but these are relatively minor efforts, at least so far.

17   See Chris Smith, *Creative Britain* (London: Faber and Faber, 1998).

18   The influence of the then Senator Aden Ridgeway on this aspect of the policy is apparent.

19   Paul Kelly, 'In Howard's image', The *Weekend Australian*, 20–21 August 2005.

20   For Howard's own explanation of what he means by this phrase, see the transcript of his address to the

Australia Day Council's Australia Day luncheon, 24 January 1997.

21 See James Curran, *The Power of Speech: Australian Prime Ministers Defining the National Image* (Melbourne: Melbourne University Press, 2004), Ch.6.

22 For example, the biography by David Barnett and Pru Goward, *John Howard: Prime Minister* (Ringwood: Viking, 1997), lists neither 'art' nor 'culture' in its index.

23 For further discussion of these and other issues under the Howard Government, see *The Howard Years*, ed. Robert Manne (Melbourne: Black Inc. Agenda, 2004).

24 See Murray Goot and Ian Watson, 'Immigration, multiculturalism and national identity', in *Australian Social Attitudes: the First Report*, ed. Shaun Wilson et al. (Sydney: UNSW Press, 2005), p.190.

25 See Richard Eckersley, *Well & Good: How We Feel and Why it Matters* (Melbourne: Text Publishing, 2004) and Clive Hamilton and Richard Denniss, *Affluenza: When Too Much is Never Enough* (Crows Nest: Allen & Unwin, 2005).

26 See also Clive Bean, 'Is there a crisis of trust in Australia?', in Wilson et al., p.131.

27 See Goot and Watson.

28 Reproduced as an appendix in Horne, pp.285–.

29 'Cruise Ship Australia', The *Bulletin*, 18 October 2005, p.42.

30 See UNESCO, *Universal Declaration on Cultural Diversity* (Paris: UNESCO, 2002).

31 David Throsby and Virginia Hollister, *Don't Give Up Your Day Job: an Economic Study of Professional Artists in Australia* (Sydney: Australia Council, 2003).

32   David Throsby and Glenn Withers, *What Price Culture?* (Sydney: Australia Council, 1984).

33   See John Holden, *Capturing Cultural Value: How Culture Has Become a Tool of Government Policy* (London: Demos, 2004).

34   Kevin F. McCarthy et al., *Gifts of the Muse: Reframing the Debate about the Benefits of the Arts* (Santa Monica: RAND Corporation, 2004).

35   See, for example, Keith Gallasch, 'Art in a Cold Climate: Rethinking the Australia Council', *Platform Papers,* no. 6 (October 2005).

36   See, for example, John Howkins, *The Creative Economy: How People Make Money from Ideas* (London: Penguin, 2001).

37   As argued by Martin Harrison, '"Our ABC" a dying culture?', *Platform Papers*, no. 1, July 2004.

38   In an interview with Ramona Koval on 'Books and Writing', ABC Radio National, 23 October 2005.

39   Guy Rundle and Max Gillies, *Your Dreaming: Poets, Pontificators and Expatriates* (Annandale: Pluto Press, 2002), pp. 45–6.

Readers' Forum

Sue Beal with some arts funding history

Keith Gallasch's 'Art in a Cold Climate: Rethinking the Australia Council' (*Platform Papers* No.6) raises many questions in his essay that I could get my teeth into but I only have the space and time to address one. I've chosen, 'Could it be that the Major Performing Arts Board skews the functioning of the Australia Council?'

I joined the Theatre Board in 1984 and the first decision made during my membership was to place a ceiling on the funds allocated to the State theatre companies. It's not unreasonable to believe that the hysteria this provoked within these institutions was a significant factor in the creation of a special place for them which would indulge their belief of artistic superiority. And Keith is absolutely right: the buffering of the large companies against critical artistic analysis is one of the many ways that the OzCo, originally envisaged as a nurturer of creativity and innovation, has transformed itself into a bureaucracy that appears to see itself primarily as a supporter of good business practice.

That the brave move to limit the profligacy of large companies may have partially contributed to them receiving even more favoured treatment than in the past does nothing to erode my pride in being associated with the attempt. The Theatre Board had a limited budget and a clear vision. The constantly increasing demands of the majors were putting more and more pressure on the ability to realise this vision. For us to be able to support the new, the difficult, the risky and the emerging we had to find a way of limiting our support of the institutional. Worthy as they might be, they weren't the only ones producing the work our Board believed it had been created to support.

My pride in being part of the decision to limit the Board's function as an agent of 'industry' assistance is balanced by my embarrassment at the part I played in elevating the performing arts to industry status. As an Actors Equity official with the best of intentions, I argued strongly for the recognition of the arts as an industry, believing that this would result in an improvement to artists' conditions. Well, it did improve the conditions of some, but it also provided the arguments used by the majors in their never-ending demands for increased support from the Theatre Board. It also paved the way for the economic rationalists who soon moved in with their mantra, 'If it can't be counted, it has no value'.

Cash flows, attendance projections, sponsorship deals, business plans, burgeoning 'infrastructure', marketing consultants, accountants negotiating with accountants—all in the name of 'best practice', and often producing bigger deficits—this became the milieu of the majors. Vision, imagination, artistic risk, innovation, experiment, obsession became peripheral. The bottom line was deified. The worst possible skewing one could imagine.

And it could have been so different. Within days of the Labor Party coming to power in 1982, Pat Galvin, the Secretary of the Department responsible for the arts, suggested to the OzCo that he could take over the funding of the majors and cocoon them in a corner of the department, give them CPI and leave them to their own devices. Thus leaving the Council to pursue its real agenda. I shamefacedly confess that I was one of those who argued against this, in hindsight, visionary proposal. The OzCo came up with a thousand reasons why they shouldn't be handed over. Of these the most honourable—and silly—was the belief that these companies would benefit from a critique of their work from an artistic perspective.

Ultimately, it was the accountants' arguments that won the day. If the OzCo lost the majors' huge funding allocation, it would also lose the statutory administrative proportion that came with their funding. Council couldn't countenance a reduction in staff and believed that it could control the majors. That's always been nonsense. The Boards of the majors have consistently demonstrated that their political astuteness is infinitely superior to that of the OzCo. They have succeeded where the OzCo has consistently failed: while most of the majors have built direct, confidential and beneficial relations with Canberra, the OzCo has never been able to achieve what should have been its primary goal—decent money for the arts—but instead spent most of its energies trying to survive threats to its own existence.

This is not really the OzCo's fault, although they could have gone about things differently. Ever since the establishment of a purportedly independent statutory central arts authority (in Sydney) the Canberra bureaucrats have been trying to regain territory they see as rightfully theirs. This struggle has never been acknowledged by either side (and possibly not even recognised by many at the OzCo). Council's attempts to align itself with Canberra were evident from the outset, when the founding Director, Jean Battersby, chose to align OzCo wages with those of the Canberra public service, rather than with those of arts workers, probably in the mistaken belief that grades would engender respect.

For the Council to have built on its original independence, and to have realised the current fantasy of being the leader of the arts, it would have had to make real from the beginning its role as the representative of the arts. What it has become is the representative of the State (nothing illustrates this better than the fact that we are all now obliged to include the Federal Government's coat of arms among our sponsor icons) and the problem with that position is that even there they are not successful. The Department of Communications, Information Technology and the Arts is the real face of government arts policy; the OzCo has been well and truly sidelined.

Jennifer Bott responds for the Australia Council

Keith Gallasch ('Art in a Cold Climate', *Platform Papers*, October 2005) uses an excellent extended metaphor of the arts sector as 'ecosystem'. It highlights the diversity and dynamism of the arts, and points to the interdependent nature of all players within the sector. But Gallasch's view of the Australia Council is a conservative one, tying us to the passive role of 'public cheque book' for the arts. And at a time when the artform silos are breaking down, Keith Gallasch is busy building walls.

If the arts sector is like an ecosystem, then the Australia Council for the Arts is an integral agent within it. We do not believe the Australia Council is the arts. We do not own the arts or seek to manage or control them, but we do have a leadership role which we exercise through financial and human resources, dialogue and research. We play a vital role in supporting the sector's growth, in fostering the relationships between different organisms and in building links to the wider social 'biosphere' that is the Australian community.

It is precisely because we are so much part of the artistic landscape that the Australia Council embarked on our first major reorganisation in 1996 and our second last year. We saw that if the arts sector was to continue to grow, new ways of supporting it were needed.

From where does growth come? From new artistic ideas and forms—and these are everywhere in the arts, not the exclusive domain of new media and hybridity. Australian works performed by the major performing arts companies increased from 75 in 1999 to 207 in 2004—which hardly tallies with Gallasch's assertion that such companies play 'a diminishing role in shaping the future of our culture'. The real issue is not stale arguments about hybrid and new media arts versus 'artforms we inherited from the nineteenth century', as Gallasch would have it, but that the Australia Council is positioned to respond to growth and change appropriately.

There is far more value in having Australia's major performing companies—its flagship theatre, dance, circus and opera companies and its orchestras—funded by the Australia Council than directly by government, as Gallasch poses. Far from being 'protected' species in the arts ecosystem, these companies are rigorously reviewed in all measures. Further, the Council's new artform directors are charged with representing their artforms across all areas of Australia Council activity, including the major performing arts, and in doing so give the Council its vital 'big picture' overview of the issues and concerns of each sector of the arts in Australia. The artificial separation of these companies from the rest of our arts infrastructure is the antithesis of the direction in which we believe these relationships should develop—artistic links, mentoring and shared resources are all possible areas of collaboration.

To suggest that an Australia Council freed of responsibility for the major performing arts companies could then magically get on with tackling 'key issues in the arts' reveals a deep misunderstanding of the Australia Council's role and the nature of the Australian arts. Why would a statutory authority give away half its budget and responsibility for key arts infrastructure? Who has decided that key issues in the arts are outside the major companies? How would the Council's role be enhanced by separating us from the artistic achievements, audience reach, profile and governance strength of the major performing arts companies? We have a duty of care for, and a commitment to add value to, arts infrastructure in Australia—it is one of our key priorities.

The Australia Council is not ambivalent about innovation; it's embedded in everything we support. For example, the Council's Theatre Board defines innovation for its grants programs as 'being intensely attuned to contemporary life to the extent that it affects the work that you make and the way that you make the work ... It means investigating, testing and taking risks'. This is a cogent reminder of our mission.

We believe we now have the right structure and processes in place to support this breadth of creativity. By supporting new media and hybrid practice across the Council's Visual Arts Board, Music Board and Inter-Arts Office, we are encouraging cross-fertilisation between all arts practices. Rather than destroying the habitat for new media and hybrid arts, as Gallasch contends, we have morphed to become more flexible in how we support it. The commitment—in funding dollars, in peer assessment, in great initiatives like Synapse, Time_Place_Space and Run_Way—remains in place.

Our support of contemporary arts practices has never been stronger, and our annual budget continues to grow. The investment in the Visual Arts and Craft Strategy, following the Myer Report, has resulted in a total of $39 million of new investment on top of existing funds to support contemporary practice. The Council's recent funding outcomes include support for the ongoing financial stability of major performing arts companies ($3.9 million) and renewed commitments to the NOISE youth arts festivals ($5 million),

Books Alive ($8 million) and Young and Emerging Artists initiative ($2.5 million), not to mention an exemption from partial indexation of all the Council's funding for the arts. None of this accords with the accusation of 'downsizing to do with less' that Gallasch would pin on the Council.

If biology shows us anything, it is that the relationships between organisms serve to create a whole that is something more than its parts. Everything is connected; nothing resides outside. The Australia Council has changed to better support and foster these connections. We have changed to ensure that Australia's artistic landscape continues to grow, for the arts and for all Australians.

Darren Tofts on charging an active circuit

In a special 2001 issue of *Artlink* magazine devoted to the 'e-volution of new media', Julianne Pierce, then director of the Australian Network for Art and Technology, observed that with 'innovation and knowledge as key buzzwords of the political agenda, it is vital that this is translated into ongoing support of cultural digital practice within this country'. Nearly five years on, this rallying of support for the emerging practice of new media arts in Australia sounds uncannily prescient in the context of Keith Gallasch's 'Art in A Cold Climate'. Pierce was writing of a cultural moment when the innovative arts practices associated with new and hybrid media were bolstered by what she calls 'an active circuit— a galvanising network of institutional advocacy, dedicated funding schemes (let alone boards), emerging spaces of exhibition and informed critical writing'. The sentiment of Gallasch's cogent account of the dissolution of the New Media Arts Board of the Australia Council is identical to Pierce's admonition. He is invoking a break in the active circuit, a circuit that has been gaining momentum but of which the work is in no way complete. The import of Gallasch's critique of the Australia Council implies the contrary.

Gallasch's metaphor of new media arts as an emerging ecology is apposite and timely. It elevates his overall critique from being an elegy or a critical rejoinder and proffers a vital portrait of the nodal components of the active circuits necessary for fostering innovation in the arts. Gallasch's attention to the discontinuation of the New Media Arts board is the occasion for a broader and insightful reflection on what it means to cultivate the arts. The initiation of dedicated funding for new media arts, such as the Australian Film Commission's No Frills Fund (1985) and the Australia Council's New Media Arts Board (1996) have been vital in sustaining a sense that media and hybrid arts are here to stay and are in no way an ephemeral movement, or minor footnote to the history of art.

Gallasch is quite right to assert that hybrid arts are informed by a range of extant aesthetic practices. He is also correct in arguing that hybridity entails unprecedented forms that require sensitive funding and curatorial protocols; not to mention the thorny issues of nomenclature and the challenges to critical practice and engaged public discourse. We have surpassed the shock of the new in relation to new media arts. However a thriving ecology must always be prepared for the surprises emergence brings. Emergence is beyond prediction and can only be recognised after the fact. Let us hope that in another five years we will not be looking back on a time of irreversible climactic change. It is hoped that Gallasch's constructive thoughts on rethinking the Australia Council will inspire a reconnection of this breach in an emerging system.

Contributors

Sue Beal

Sue Beal has spent thirty years working in the arts supporting, mostly, individual artists and small companies. She is now the manager of the City of Melbourne's Arts House Program, which provides a comprehensive program of support to artists from creative conception to delivery of original work.

Jennifer Bott

Jennifer Bott is Chief Executive Officer, Australia Council for the Arts.

Darren Tofts

Darren Tofts is Associate Professor of Media & Communications, Swinburne University of Technology, Melbourne. His most recent book is *Interzone: Media Arts in Australia* (London: Thames & Hudson 2005).

Subscribe to **Platform Papers**

Individual recommended retail price: $13.95

Have the papers delivered quarterly to your door:
4 ISSUES FOR $55.00 INCLUDING POSTAGE WITHIN AUSTRALIA

To Currency House Inc.
Please start this subscription from this issue/the next issue.

Name_____

_____

Address_____

_____

__

State _____ Postcode _____

Email _____

Telephone _____

Please make cheques payable to Currency House Inc.

Or charge: ___ Mastercard ___ Bankcard ___ Visa

Card no. ___ ___ ___ ___   ___ ___ ___ ___

___ ___ ___ ___   ___ ___ ___ ___   Expiry date

CURRENCY **H**OUSE

Fax this form to: Currency House Inc. at 02 9319 3649

Or post to: PO Box 2270, Strawberry Hills NSW 2012 Australia